T0065595

FREE *with* WORDS

—— Selected Poems by ——

Abenaa Kyeremeh

authorHOUSE®

AuthorHouse™ UK
1663 Liberty Drive
Bloomington, IN 47403 USA
www.authorhouse.co.uk
Phone: 0800.197.4150

Published by AuthorHouse 05/18/2015

ISBN: 978-1-5049-3804-4 (sc)
ISBN: 978-1-5049-3827-3 (e)

Print information available on the last page.

This book is printed on acid-free paper.

To anyone who has ever suffered with
depression and felt like giving up.

And to anyone who has ever been sectioned under the
Mental Health Act or detained in a psychiatric hospital.

2 Corinthians 4:8–13 (NKJV)
'We are hard pressed on every side yet not crushed.
We are perplexed but not in despair; persecuted but
not forsaken; struck down but not destroyed.'

Contents

Acknowledgements

Firstly, a massive thank you goes out to the Almighty God for giving me the gift, talent, and ability to write straight from the heart. Thanks to my biological father for encouraging me to read and write when I was a child, and thanks to my mother for believing in me and supporting me. Love and respect to the rest of my family all over the world. I am very grateful to Mr Flynn, who was one of my teachers at Vittoria Primary School in Islington, London. He was one of the best teachers I ever had, and I appreciate the fact that he encouraged his students to be creative and study hard.

I must also acknowledge Helen Yendall, my tutor from the Writers Bureau, for her advice and support while I was taking the Art of Poetry course. Thanks to everyone at Author House Publishers. The late, great Emily Brontë deserves some credit, because in the year 2000 I discovered one of her books, and reading it inspired me to write, too.

I would also like to thank everyone I have met throughout my life who has had some kind of impact on me, the main one being Jesus Christ. Hallelujah.

Introduction

Free with Words is an elaborate book of poems written between the years 2000 and 2015. The book covers eleven different topics with an interesting, eclectic mix of poetry. This book is aimed at those interested in reading something fresh and exciting, though it is the author's intention that anyone who has suffered or is currently suffering from depression will be encouraged by reading this book.

Mental illness is something which affects many people all over the world, for various reasons. We now live in a world that at times can be very stressful, with people finding themselves under pressure. In some parts of the world, there is often a lack of community spirit. Society has now changed, with more and more people suffering from isolation, loneliness, and depression. These factors can have an impact on our mental health and well-being.

If we look at the Christian perspective regarding the future of society, then we can look to a scripture in the Bible (2 Timothy 3:1–4, New King James Version); this particular verse speaks about how we are living in the end days, and that people will be lovers of themselves. It also says that men will be despisers of good. However, it is important to note that the Christian perspective also includes optimism, hope, and encouragement. This is because Jesus Christ, known as the Saviour, came to give life, and give it abundantly. Christians believe that Jesus will one day return, and there will eventually be peace on earth, though in the meantime, it is possible for us humans to have part of God's Holy Spirit inside of us. It could be said that having faith can give a person inner peace, strength, and determination. Also, having the belief that God can heal people and perform miracles in their lives could be comforting to them.

Obviously, not everybody believes in Jesus Christ or believes that God exists. Also, there are many people in the world who practice different faiths and believe in things other than Jesus Christ. Something that many people would agree with is that there are many problems in the world. People are looking for solutions to their problems as well as answers to certain questions. Many people in the world are suffering and feel that they have no one to turn to. Whether Christian or atheist, it is important to appreciate the importance of the power of love.

Free with Words is an honest viewpoint, coming from an individual who has a vast amount of experience within the British mental health system. This book not only deals with the subject of mental illness, it also discusses common issues such as faith, love, hope, and pain. It is the type of book that can be opened at any page, giving an intriguing read and enlightenment, on issues that affect most of us at some stage in our lives. Most of the poems within this book contain an unconventional style of writing poetry, hence the name of the book: *Free with Words*.

Selected Poems

FAITH

HOPE

LOVE

INSPIRATION

WISDOM

PAIN

HEALTH

ME

EXPERIENCE

LONDON

AFRICA

MISCELLANEOUS

Faith

1. Who You Know

I never used to believe in the saying
'It's not what you know but who you know,'
until I started praying many years ago.

Someone found me and set me free.
He turned me into a new person.
He helped me to see.

He gave me a new life and a will to survive,
a new meaning and feeling;
it's great to be breathing.

My life is in God's hands.
He has great and wonderful plans.
It's a relief, that I am blessed beyond belief.

So now I march forwards.
I'm a Christian soldier; I will fight the good
fight of faith, even when I get older.

An omnipotent God, whom I have come to know,
Jesus Christ is my Saviour
and it's Him whom I will follow.

2. The Second Coming

The great Messiah:
He's going to take some of us higher,
up to heaven,
so come on, sisters and brethren.

Jesus is not a liar.
He is the truth and the way.
It's up to us where we end up
in this game of life that we play.

He walked the earth before
and came for both the rich and the poor.
He's coming back again
with the ability to be our best friend.

The world needs a solution
for the trouble that we face.
So it's encouraging to know that
Jesus can take us to a much better place.

Reality and certainty with great possibility.
Assurance regarding God's performance.
Revelation, revolution,
restoration, reformation.

We human beings can have hope in Jesus Christ.
The Holy Spirit is with us
and can help to open up our eyes.
Open our eyes, so that we can see the light.

History was made when Jesus rose from the grave.
Now he lives, so that we can be saved.
Jesus has the ability to guide us every day.
We can rest assured that we have the victory, come what may.

One day He will return in His full splendour,
our majesty the king.
This gives us hope and confidence
in the blessings that He brings.

Though let us not forget, so that we will have no regrets,
there is a heaven and there is a hell.
If we do not know now, one day we will be able to tell.
Let's give our hearts to the Lord, where great treasures can be stored.

Judgement day is approaching.
Let's hope that we all get to a better place.
Jesus will be seen in His full glory.
We will see him face to face.

3. Come on, Jesus!

Come on, Jesus, come on, Jesus!
Show your power, light the fire.
See my need; help me breathe.
I need more strength to keep on going.
Holy Spirit, keep on flowing.

Lord, have mercy and keep me strong,
though in the past I have done some wrongs.
Your love and saving grace will put a smile upon my face.
The little that I know
will grow, grow, and grow.

Every day I want to know you more.
I will knock on your door.
I will seek your face in the secret place.
Let your will be done.
Lord, let your Holy Spirit come.

You reign and are in complete control;
may your power and love continue to unfold.
You know just what I need;
help me to continue to believe.
Take away all of my fears and wipe away all of my tears.

I believe that one day you will return
to carry me away.
This gives me hope for a brighter future
and helps me to get through each day.
Come on, Jesus, come on, Jesus!

4. The Blood of Jesus

I see visions of blood.
Is it the blood of Jesus?
I don't really know,
but I see a red flow.

Initially, I felt fear,
and my eyes shed tears,
but that was many years ago;
now I still continue to see the flow.

I'm no longer afraid.
I know that Jesus rose from the grave.
He paid the ultimate price
by giving His life as a sacrifice.

I see visions of blood.
Is it the blood of Jesus?
What I think I see
has the power to set me free.

The blood of Jesus can cleanse me
and wash away my sin.
The blood of Jesus can strengthen me,
give me victory, and enable me to win.

The pain that Jesus suffered,
when He was crucified on the cross,
means that we can now be saved
and not be lost.

I see visions of blood.
Is it the blood of Jesus?
I see visions of blood.
I cry out, 'Jesus, Jesus, Jesus.'

5. Essence of Perfection

The ingredients are fresh;
there is everything I need.
I want to make a sweet life;
I'm determined to succeed.

I've put in some faith and
mixed it with God's love.
Also happiness, peace, and joy
heaven sent from up above.

As much Holy Spirit as God
can kindly spare. Compassion,
forgiveness, and patience are
added; there's joy in abundance
everywhere.

I need a little something extra.
It has to be some kind of hope.
This will keep me going from
day to day and, in difficult times,
help me to cope.

I must not forget the essence
of perfection – it's hard work,
I have to admit. I aim to strive
every day, and if I make mistakes,
I will adhere to God's correction.

6. The Fight of My Life

I want to fight and be strong,
fight to belong,
fight for peace,
be an evangelist on the streets.

Fight against injustice,
put my faith into practice.
I want to rise to the challenge
without taking revenge.

My enemies will fall,
and I will stand tall;
when I'm under attack,
spiritually speaking, I'll fight back.

When the darkness appears
God's light will take away my fears.
When things aren't going my way
I'll dig deep and continue to pray.

This battle is not for the weak.
I train hard and hope to seek
my reward at the end of the fight.
So I'll continue with power and might.

Hope

7. Better Days Are on the Way

Is it true what some people say?
That change is coming,
with better days on the way?
I think it's true.
God knows what I've have been through.

Some days have been a struggle
when my mind has been puzzled.
But I hold on tight to my faith
as I look forward to one day
walking through heaven's gates.

Not long now,
soon we are going to see the king;
oh, what joy that will bring.
God is good all the time.
I think about Him and can't help but smile.

8. The Journey

I am getting there
by the grace of God.
I'm making progress;
thank you, Lord.
Sometimes it feels like I'm going backwards
and going through the same old thing.
Then my faith in God sinks in.
In fact, I am moving forwards,
spiritually speaking.
I am saved,
and born again,
on my way to the promised
land: heaven.

9. The Voice from Within

I cannot put on an act and be who I used to be.
The person I used to be no longer exists;
she has gone for good, and I knew she would.
The reason why I knew she would go
is that she was unhappy, if the truth were known.
She searched for years to find the meaning,
the meaning of life to improve her feelings.
She looked left, she looked right, she looked up, and she looked down;
she searched all different places, even other people's faces.
She saw other people enjoying their lives and said,
'What's wrong with me? I deserve to survive.
I do not want to struggle to find happiness.
There must be a way that my mind can have rest.'

She carried on searching to find what she knew
would make life worth living, something true.
The search took her to places she did not know,
it was not quite where she was supposed to go.
When she got there, she said,
'Well, is this it, then? Is this what I have been looking for?'
Obviously not, she felt and knew that she needed more.
Something told her deep from within,
'You keep on searching, and you will win.
Keep searching, keep trying, do what needs to be done;
one day you will be happy and you will have won.
What you have been after for years and years,
don't give up now; keep moving, my dear.'

So she kept on going, through thick and thin;
she continued to listen to the voice from within.
Some days were like battles and became harder and harder;
the road got rough and she said, 'How much further?'
Sweat turned to tears, tears turned to anger,
panic set in when she met a stranger.
A stranger called Satan, she had not met before,
hard to describe, but felt him for sure.
Feelings of sadness, pain, and confusion.
The voice she had been used to suddenly changed.
'What's happened to me? This feels awfully strange.
I do not like this, and if I have a choice,
I prefer to hear the sound of the other voice, of course.'

She knew what to do, it was perfectly clear:
she chose to listen to the voice she preferred to hear.
The voice which gave hope and answers to solutions
became louder and sorted out any confusion.
Then came a stage in this young woman's life
that began to explain what the whole thing was about.
The search, the battle, the sleepless nights,
the answers to questions, reasons, no doubts.
She knew it; she knew that this day would come,
what she had been looking for all along.
Now that she has it, she knows it for sure, for that person is me,
unhappy no more. This story explains what I've been through
why my old life is old and my new one is new.

I cannot act and be who I used to be.
I have moved on; I am now free.
The voice from within is what has changed me.
The voice now is so loud; I can't say I don't hear it.
It's loud, it's clear, and it's why I'm still here.
The old me has gone; she has gone for good.
I had hope; I had faith and believed that she would.
Never again now will I choose to ignore,
the loud voice within me as I did before.
It speaks for a reason, a purpose, with feeling;
that's what gives my life it's value and meaning.
The meaning of life is so very important; it's what I need to know.
Now with confidence and enthusiasm, it's onward and forward I go.

(Written in 2000, after I became a Christian.)

10. Breakthrough

I haven't cried for ages. I'm really doing well,
considering; recently, it felt as though
I was going through hell. Now I'm out of the wilderness
and trying to live life to the full.
Though I have to stop and think to myself,
why is life at times so cruel?

Back then, I was totally lost.
I needed some type of direction;
afraid and insecure, I also needed protection.
I reached out for help but had no other human but myself.
Days seemed dark and cold, then things got worse
as the difficulties of life began to unfold.

But that's over now, and it's time for a fresh start;
life has become so much more different.
Now I have real joy in my heart.
So I rejoice at the fact that I'm alive.
I've developed great determination
with a strong will to survive.

I'm breaking through obstacles that were once in place.
My swagger says it all, along with the big grin on my face.
Remnants of the past are gladly disappearing;
a taste of what's to come gives me a satisfied feeling.
Breakthrough – I've broken through and have the cuts and scars;
my healing is taking place, and I have come quite far.

The road that I have travelled has brought me a mighty long way.
I do not want to go back to that place where I came from,
I honestly have to say.
So it's shoulders back, chest forward, and head held high;
with great determination,
it will only be tears of joy that I cry.

11. Seize the Day

Do not hesitate or procrastinate;
you only live once, so take full advantage of every given chance.
Seize the day, come what may.

Be a real go-getter; be gutsy and sure.
There is no one like you; no one has lived your life before.
Always be grateful for what you have; be forgiving and try to love.

Problems will come and then they will go,
though try to be optimistic and look forward to tomorrow.
Be joyful and be hopeful, though never too boastful.

Whatever the weather, believe that things can get better.
Try to smile every day; have faith and believe and pray.
Keep on moving, not losing but improving.

Take pleasure in knowing that as you are growing,
you can become wiser each day.
Strive to be excellent at what you do; success can also apply to you.

12. Mind over Matter

Put your mind over what is the matter;
fill your brain with food that will help you get
intellectually fatter.
Focus on positivity
not negativity.

No matter what the problem or the situation,
there is always hope;
if you do not give in, you won't give up.
Try not to lose hope, because if you do,
you will not reach your full potential.

Just imagine, one day, being very influential
with plenty of credentials.
Have strong faith in what you believe.
Have no doubts regarding what you are
capable of achieving.

Never put limitations on yourself,
but push yourself every day.
Try not to say, 'I can't do this, or that,'
unless the thing that you are saying no to
is not good for you.

13. Saved

Saved from a hellish grave;
back then, I didn't know the right way to behave.
If I knew then what I know now,
It would have saved a lot of trouble someway, somehow.

Saved from a painful death;
I was holding on to my last breath.
My chest was getting tighter and tighter, but I am a fighter.
Struggling to survive, I got down on my knees and prayed to stay alive.

Saved from being knocked down by a car;
I did not see it coming from afar.
Smack, bang in the side of my body. I didn't fall to the ground,
but I felt like wobbly jelly.

Saved from committing suicide;
thank God that Jesus Christ was on my side.
I've been saved from sin and death.
I've been saved from sin and death.

14. Revolution

This is it. I'm ready; the revolution has begun.
Transformation is taking place;
it feels like I've already won.
No longer will I put up with oppression and injustice.
I will fight until the end, but I'm not out to get revenge.

I will not fight physically,
though I'm fed up with other people's hostility.
There's only so much I can take; I don't want to break.
I'll be confident and brave. I'll try to forgive
and, with inner peace, live.

There doesn't need to be too many to start a revolution.
One person's voice can be strong,
if it shouts loud enough for long enough.
I've been shouting for years, and I've shed many tears.
Now the revolution has begun; some people better run.

I've been pushed around for far too long
and felt as though I didn't belong.
Now I'm wiser; I had to learn the hard way.
I knew I had strength to make it someday.
I'm now receiving my pay, without any delay.

I'm making progress, moving upwards and forwards.
This battle is not for the weak; I'm reaching my peak.
I'm full of optimism; no room for pessimism.
I'm hopeful all the way,
determined every day.

I won't be overly confident
or too big for my boots;
I must stay level headed and not forget my roots.
I'll try my best to be able to stand out from the rest,
There's an uprising that's suddenly occurring.

I've failed at some things before but didn't give up.
I got back on my feet and went back for more.
Now I've learnt to take the rough with the smooth.
I've found my own unique style
and personal groove.

The revolution has begun,
now I'm shining like the sun.
The past is right behind me, and I want everyone to see.
The words that now need to be spoken are
that a freedom fighter has finally awoken.

Love

15. This Love Thing is deep

I cannot sleep. I cannot eat.
I cannot walk or talk the way I used to.
It's because of you.
When I see you, I feel as though I will fall to the ground.
I'm so nervous and shy; I can't utter a sound.
This love thing certainly is profound.

You have the ability to make me melt;
this type of love, I'm sure I have never felt.
I think of you when you are not around.
I bet I even talk about you in my sleep;
am I getting in too deep?
This love, I want to keep.

16. Instant Attraction

It's not all about looks,
but what I could see looked
very attractive to me.
It's not all about charm,
though the way you spoke,
I thought this is no ordinary bloke.

Did you see me as a beautiful woman,
someone who deserves
to be treated with respect?
Because most men I've met, I now choose to forget.
You told me that I had beautiful eyes.
That came as a big surprise.

Just because I said yes to the others,
I had to tell you to go.
You simply asked me out on a date,
but were you genuine or were you fake?
I guess I'll never know
because now it's probably too late.

The instant attraction was learning to love
the woman beneath the veil.
I need to learn to love myself,
so that I can also love somebody else.
Then maybe if we meet again
the attraction will not fail.

17. God's Unconditional Love

You lay down no conditions when you love me;
your unconditional love expects nothing back in return.
I continue to learn that God is love.
You love us all,
regardless of what we've done, even if we sin and fall.
When we make mistakes in life,
which is something we often do,
you are able to forgive us, if we repent and turn to you.
Your love sets no boundaries;
you don't discriminate.
Whether black or white, you never hate.
I love the way that you love
me, the way that you do.
I've never been loved by anyone like you before;
now I want you more and more.

18. The Difference between Love and Hate

Love is like a bud that blossoms
into a beautiful flower.
Hate is like a weed, and when watered,
it feeds from the greed
and the need to destroy the trees.
I am a tree that bears beautiful flowers.
I am a tree that stands strong and towers.
My flowers are now dying, and I cannot help crying.
My buds are still blooming, but hate is still looming.

The difference between love and hate is that love never fails!

Inspiration

19. Free with Words

Confidently, I use my vocabulary with great intensity,
frequently conveying and saying that I am free with words.
Contemplation of writing, to the best of my ability,
without any notion of insecurity.
No messing about with words; when I write, I'm free like a bird.
I hope and pray that one day, my poems will be read throughout
the world and heard.

My chains have been broken; now there's no holding back,
poetry in motion without any lack.
Learning along the way, to cope with taking flak.
My imagination runs to the inner depths of my being;
my senses come alive, this helps me to survive.
My mind is open to the welcoming presence of ideas.
This gives me great potential and wipes away all traces of fear.

With anticipation and great expectation,
I move to another dimension and a deeper level of understanding.
Prolifically and profoundly, I try to use my intelligence wisely.
No inhibition or limitation regarding the ability to be free with words.
So by using my initiative, I gravitate towards an element of
deep probability. I'm able to achieve anything I put my mind to.
My thought patterns react to my natural characteristics.

I literally flex my muscles, exercising and working out
the best way that I can write.
I'm thinking and believing that I am capable of succeeding.
The excitement grows;
the writing flows, and I know that
I'm onto a good thing. This is something big,
so I continue to dig to test my capabilities.

I stretch and expand with my pen in my hand.
The paper is crisp; this I refuse not to miss.
Rhythmically, the ink dances, and I feel like taking chances.
I go that extra mile, though sometimes I rest a little while.
I then get up and carry on again in ample style.
I wait to see what could possibly happen next.
Writing is one of the things that I love to do best.

I feel great at the prospect of conquering one of my fears.
I will not develop a severe case of writer's block.
I refuse to get trapped and locked into a negative mindset and believe
that I'm incapable of writing poetry.
Even with restrictions or restraints on me, I am
Free with words.
Free as a bird.

20. Strength

I will soar like an eagle and run like a cheetah,
walk with finesse.
I will pass the test.

God gives me strength to do all things.
That's why, with each new day,
I'm able to sing.

Light of the world,
Jesus shines through the darkness.
Sparkle and glow, give me power to grow.

You go, God, you go.
You go to and through
You breathe on me and help me feel free.

21. Be Encouraged

Be encouraged
to use your courage;
proceed to achieve.
Believe you can succeed.

Have motivation
and inspiration;
acquire perseverance
with determination.

Those days when
you're downhearted
and your hope
has departed,

be encouraged
to use your courage;
proceed to achieve.
Believe you can succeed.

Have confidence and faith;
go ahead and be brave.
You only have one life to live,
so see how much you can give.

Think back to those things
that you once thought
you would never achieve.
Let that now motivate you to believe.

As your future unfolds,
stick to your dreams
and goals; hold tight
and never let go.

Be encouraged
to use your courage;
proceed to achieve.
Believe you can succeed.

Where you want to go in life
and what you want to do,
few people may have made it before
but you are not them, you are you.

You may have been discouraged in the past;
your confidence at present could be low,
but think of the dreams and hopes that you have.
Have faith for a brighter tomorrow.

Be encouraged
to use your courage;
proceed to achieve.
Believe you can succeed.

22. Brothers and Sisters

Don't' be a fool, play it real cool.
Don't be afraid; remember that Jesus rose from the grave.
He was crucified for me and for you,
for all of us, not just a mere few.
Reflect on the good times that you have had in your life;
don't only think about trouble and strife.

Believe that there is always light at the end of the tunnel.
Though sometimes it seems like
you are going down a never-ending, slippery funnel.
The way out seems to get tighter and tighter,
but hold on, brothers and sisters, and just tell yourself that
'I am a fighter, a fighter.'

Hold onto your faith, because God strengthens the brave.
Never give up, and do not give in.
Believe in yourself when others will not;
trust in the Lord when others have forgot.
Brothers and sisters, rise to the challenge;
be the best that you can possibly be.

One day, we will be free!

23. You Go, Girl!

Cheer up, girl, why do you look so sad?
Lift your head up, darling, things aren't that bad.
Believe in yourself, and things will start to happen.
Great things are coming your way;
it might be tomorrow if not today.

Don't you realise what you've got inside?
You have a great and beautiful mind.
So you go, girl, rise and shine.
Things may get difficult sometimes,
but have faith that eventually, everything will be fine.

You will face battles and challenges, yes,
but if you try your hardest, you're sure to pass the test.
You may fail at some things, but you'll learn
from your mistakes. You have strength and power
within; you'll win whatever it takes.

24. Run for Your Life

Run for your life.
Run to Jesus Christ.
Go and get your prize,
those who are wise.

Don't settle for mediocrity;
go for something with superiority.
Jesus has great things for us all.
He enables us to rise when we fall.

Run like you've never run before;
ask, seek, and knock on heaven's door.
There's life in abundance, free for all.
We'll receive it in Jesus name if we call.

If you want to be a winner, then you must
run the race. Show great discipline and you
can win. Be determined, have faith, and see
what positivity that will bring.

The real battles in our lives begin when we start to fight,
fight, against the challenges that we face.
Look fear straight in the eye.
You can succeed if you try.

Above all else, believe in God and yourself,
and things will start to happen. Don't look
back or look down. One day you'll get what
you want and wear a crown.

Wisdom

25. What Is Wisdom?

What is wisdom? Do you have a place?
I've often heard that you come from God.
Is it His amazing grace?
Is it possible to see His face?

What is wisdom?
Is it to know what's right from wrong?
Or to know that we have power, coming from a source
that's very strong?

What is wisdom?
I really need to know.
I heard that you can get it from a book
many years ago.

What is wisdom?
Does it have a number, is there a sequence,
or could I write it in a letter
to make me feel better?

What is wisdom?
Could someone tell me please?
I know that there is an answer
that will satisfy my needs.

26. I Have Something on My Mind

I have something on my mind.
You may call it confusion.
The drugs don't work, at times, darkness lurks
and forms strange illusions.

You say that I am sick.
I say that you are thick.
You say that I can't cope,
then it's as if you tie my hands with rope.

Set me free.
Let me be
me, me,
me.

I have something on my mind
more than just a brain.
I'm often treated like
I am insane.

Something on my mind
will one day tell the story
of how I was right about what was wrong.
Then God's justice will bring me glory.

27. Studious

Crumpled pieces of paper lay sprawled
across the living room floor. At the moment,
they're being ignored, waiting to be gathered
together, picked up, and thrown away.
But not today, because this is the room of an artist.
A poet, a student, ambitious and prudent.

A chip off the old writer's block patiently waits
to create a masterpiece, a piece of work
that will surpass all previous ones.
There is passion and desire, a heart filled with fire,
a will to learn something new
and be the best at what I can do.

I'm refining my craft, and I want to improve.
Being true to myself; there's nobody that I'm
trying to delude. I want wisdom, knowledge,
and understanding. The desire to know more,
no floundering. I have aspirations to publish
a great book. I've made a start on my work of art.

I have great ambition and wouldn't mind recognition.
I feel that I have something important to prove,
but also nothing to lose. I don't mind being called studious;
it really isn't ludicrous.
A gift is what I feel that I have.
It needs to be used, not wasted or abused.

28. Wickedness

The wicked people are getting on my nerves.
Why oh why can't goodness be preserved?
It's such a shame. It makes me angry and causes me pain,
but I always remember to call upon Jesus Christ's name.
My frustration is strong, but Jesus is stronger.
With this in mind, I do not have to wonder,
wonder about what will happen to the wicked.
For the wicked are reserved for the day of doom.
In the kingdom that's to come, I don't think that wickedness
will have any room.

29. Get Ready for the Truth

People, get ready, for the truth is on its way;
no more room for lying. It's almost judgement day.

We cannot comprehend exactly what will happen,
but it will be fantastic, that much I can fathom.

Smack in the face to expose our disgrace,
we will be lying on the floor until we lie no more.

People, get ready, for the truth is on its way;
the best way that we can prepare, is to have faith in God and pray.

30. The Imagination

The pollution has concentrated the dilution.

The dilution has merged with the confusion.

The confusion is eliminating the proposition.

The proposition is demanding a solution.

The solution is regarding a condition.

The condition is responsible for imagination.

The imagination is a result of the …

Pain

31. Do You Care?

Do you care?
Yes you, the one who caused me misery,
for I cared so much, but you just did not see.

Do you care?
Yes you, the one who caused me to despair
because I cared. I did and thought of you in my prayers.

Were you there?
Yes you, when I was lying on the ground.
I was there for sure, and you could not be found.

Where were you?
Yes you, when there was no one else around.
I looked but could not see you, and I did not hear a sound.

Do you care?
Yes you, the one who said you cared so much,
the same one who said that I could trust.

What happened to the care in you?
Tell me what happened; where did it go to?
If you did not care, then why did you dare to say, 'Oh yes, I do'?

To care means to share your love; it's not something
to be taken for granted. To care means to show it and grow it
like a beautiful flower that's been planted.

Did you care? Do you care? Hello, hello; yes, you.
Hello, hello; look, I'm not talking to myself,
or am I?

Have you disappeared like everyone else?
You have gone;
well, I guess that says it all.

I guess that is my answer.
You have disappeared, and I'm left with my tears;
you were not even there when I was crying.

Do you care?

32. I'm Drowning

I'm drowning in my own mess.
How do I cope and get out of this distress?
I'm not floating; no, I'm not coping or even joking.

Is there no way out?
How much louder do I have to shout?
What can I do? Time is running out.

Too many regrets and quite a few doubts.
I never knew that life could be so tough,
though I have heard that with the smooth also comes the rough.

Good childhood memories come flooding back.
That was a time when it did not feel like I was under attack.
Life was so much fun then; it all seemed like just a game, very little pain.

Back then, I thought that things would remain the same.
But now, everything has changed.
Oh, the shame.

Who will pull me out of this hell hole that I have made?
I want to stand up and be tall, bold, and brave.
I'm in too deep and cry out for help as I weep.

33. Goodbye, Sunshine

Summer's gone.
And so have you.
I thought you were the one,
but you were too good to be true.

Now the rain pours,
and being here is lonely.
I don't want to go outdoors.
That's why I wanted you only.

The wind blows strongly.
Brown crisp leaves fall from the trees.
I need someone to comfort me.
Oh, how I miss the summer breeze.

Shorter, colder days,
I need a warm embrace.
With winter on its way,
I need a smile upon my face.

Goodbye, sunshine.
I've lost two things
that were both sublime.
I miss the sun up above and the man that I loved.

How do I carry on anymore?
The snow will soon be falling.
Will you ever come back to knock on my door?
It's my name that I want you to be calling.

Where are you now, with another woman?
Are you feeling the beat of somebody else's heart?
I have to get over you; you will be forgiven.
I'll find new love and a fresh start?

My heart feels frozen inside my chest.
My body feels heavy, especially at night.
I need some warmth and someone to caress,
but I now realise you were not Mr Right.

Why can I not get you out of my mind?
I feel quite silly that I often think of you.
Is it because there is no one else I can find?
I can picture your face; I don't know what to do.

I will save my love for somebody who will
respect me even more.
So please don't attempt to come
knocking on my front door.

34. Loneliness

She often goes out on her own
then comes home to an empty flat.
She checks for messages on her phone,
then takes off her coat, scarf, and hat.

She eats on her own, her favourite vegetable dish,
as she wonders what she'll do in the evening.
To have company and more fun is her wish,
but she's been trying for years without succeeding.

She tries to sleep in her double bed,
but there's a draft coming through the closed
window and condensation on the inside
window ledge.

Racing thoughts begin to bombard her mind.
She tosses and turns and then begins to weep;
negativity and distress is all she can find.
She feels her life's a mess and it's much too deep.

It's three in the morning; where can she go?
Churches aren't even open; every place is closed.
The heating isn't working properly; she sits feeling cold.
Things begin to get worse as suicidal thoughts unfold.

She shouts, she swears, her honest feelings she bares.
She tries to pray, but things just aren't working out today;
she's a Christian, oh yes, and she knows that she's
blessed.

But the loneliness is like torture, ripping flesh from
the bone. That's why sometimes she feels like
just ending it all. What should she do?
How can she continue to go on?

She managed to get through the night, though it sure was
a tough fight. Faith and prayer pulled her through;
she knew what to do. She dug deep within her soul and,
eventually, accomplished a positive goal.

35. Why I Cry

I cry because I hurt when people treat me like dirt.
I weep because the pain cuts so deep, and out of my eyes,
the tears seep.

I cry when people betray me and use me, with their terrible
cruelty. Tears roll down my cheeks, and sometimes
I cannot speak.

All I can do at that point in time is to express
what I feel; it's real,
and the pain is mine.

So I'll cry until my tears dry up. I'll cry until I've had enough.
Then I'll laugh because I'm supposed to.
To everything there is a season, and everything happens for a reason.

Health

36. Sectioned

(under the Mental Health Act)

Sectioned yet again, how many times now?
Sometimes it makes me stop and think to myself, but how?
Why me? What did I do wrong?
Should I have done this, or should I have done that?
Is someone else to blame?
Is this some kind of sick joke,
or is it a game?

When will all of this end?
Psychiatric hospitals are not my best friend,
neither are they my worst,
but sometimes, I feel that I will burst, and sometimes I do.
Burst into a flood of tears;
I think to myself that one of my biggest fears
is to be sectioned yet again.

Then I think to myself, Stop, hold on,
I am a child of God.
'God has not given us a spirit of fear
but of power and of love
and of a sound mind'
So I come out of hospital and start again
with great determination, my life will not remain the same.

37. Dear Jesus

Once again, I have been sectioned under the Mental Health Act.
However, I shall stay strong and I shall not fear,
because I know, Lord Jesus,
that you are always here.

I think of all the many great things which you have done
for me in the past. It gives me hope and assurance
that whatever difficult thing I am going through at the moment
cannot and will not last.

I love you so much, Jesus, and I know that I can depend upon you
to get me out of the difficulties that I go through.
I often think to myself, what if I was in the same situation
and did not have you?

I hope that someday, I will be able to put all of this behind me
and never return to a psychiatric hospital again.
But in the meantime, continue to guide,
direct, and protect me.

Continue to strengthen me, bless me,
and fill me with your precious Holy Spirit.
Take full control of my life, Lord, and I will never forget
that you will always be the lover of my soul.

Thank you.

(This poem was written while I was in hospital on 27 July 2010.)

38. Mr and Ms Psychology

Mr and Ms Psychology,
you think you know me well.
Well, I have some news for you:
you will never be able to tell.
You try to study my mind, to see what you can find,
then you give me medication in strong doses,
then you make your wrong diagnoses.

Mr and Ms Psychology,
who or what is it that gives you the right
to do what you do?
Is it your psychology degree
that makes you think that you can judge me?
Just you wait and see, what will eventually happen to me,
Mr and Ms Psychology.

39. Wrongly Diagnosed

A change is coming, it has to be said.
I refuse to accept that I have schizo-affective disorder in my head.
A change is coming; I know it for sure.
I feel so strongly about it, like never before.

God is a healer; He's not a drug dealer.
I'm being forced to take medication, and I feel that it's unfair.
Some health professionals have told me that I will be on it forever.
They think that they are so clever.

Some doctors think that they can control
me and think they know my destiny.
Well, God is my creator, and He knows me better than anybody.
God knows, if I have been wrongly diagnosed.

40. Side Effects

The prescribed drugs that she is forced to take
have been causing her side effects.
She's been popping pills for years,
And she has many regrets.

Haloperidol, Piportil, Droperidol, Aripiprizole.
Sodium Valporate, Zuclopenthixol Deconote.
Chlorpromazine, Procyclidine, Carbomazipine, Sertraline.
Olanzipine, Diazepam.

Doctors have tried her on all the medications listed above.
This is when the push, comes to shove.
When she refuses the medication, doctors threaten to section her.
They then place her on a community treatment order.

Every four weeks, she has a depot injection
in her bum; this is certainly no fun.
Doctors say it's to help her
and for mental illness to deter.

She's had painful lumps in her breasts
caused by the side effects.
At times she feels tired because the medication sedates.
It also makes her overweight.

She's been told by her local GP,
that the depot injection could be the cause
of problems with her memory.
Then there is the so called 'care in the community.'

There's discontentment regarding the NHS
and the way that she's being treated.
Though she stands firm with inner faith,
believing that God will keep her brave and safe.

It's no surprise that she's been in hospital so
many times, feeling ill; with their psychological
experiments, she's forced to relent, as they treat
her against her will.

The system is trying to make her go mad;
it may sound hard to believe, because it's
so sad. But she knows what they have done.
This is no game; she's certainly not dumb.

She's not afraid to speak up for herself regarding
the way in which some doctors practice. She writes
poems and reports; sometimes inconceivably, she
resorts to find the right way in which to gain justice.

41. Freedom from Depression

What do I do when there is no hope?
My life seems to be going down a slippery slope.
I feel so anxious and so lost,
I then begin to live my life at a ridiculous cost.
My friends are far and few; I just don't know what to do.
I feel there's no way out.
I begin to scream and shout.
Tears, fears, pain, strain.

Depression sinks in;
I begin to sink because I'm unable to swim.
I fall to my knees and cry out,
'Lord, help me please.
I need a solution; I cannot take any more confusion,
confusion in my head; I don't want to end up dead.'
Soon I feel comfort, and then I feel love.
Now I know that there is a God that exists up above.

The depression has gone.
I feel that I have won,
won the battle, won the fight;
the victory is mine, now everything is fine.
I will never forget the God who pulled me through,
when I was at my lowest point and didn't know what to do.
God came to my rescue when no one else could,
so now I thank Him every day because He's been so good.

42. Healing

Healing.
It's what God can do, regarding the pain
that we sometimes go through.
Spiritual, physical, or emotional, pain can come in all different ways.
Though what does not kill you only makes you stronger,
I have heard many people say.
But you feel that pain, and you want to shout;
the ordeal is so intense, and out of your eyes, tears gush out.
The anguish, the torment, the pressure and distress,
confusion, sorrow, and oh, the sadness.

It feels like torture and makes you think,
what am I on this earth for?
You want to run because it feels as though you're the only one,
the only one who feels pain, and it seems like you are going insane.
You turn to people for some help and support,
but in the process you end up worse and also get cut short.
That pain is so intense and almost cuts through your heart;
when will all this end, and how did it start?
Seconds, minutes, hours, and days, you believe that there's some hope,
so you carry on and pray.

The prayers don't always get answered straight away;
you continue to struggle every day.
The odds seem stacked against you;
you think to yourself, is all of this actually true?
You begin to deteriorate and, eventually, infuriate.
But that faith deep inside your inner being gives you strength
and encouragement to keep breathing and living.
Some people do not live to see another day;
God gives and also takes away.
Will you be someone Jesus heals today?

43. Get Fit!

I only have one body,
so I have to look after it.
It's time to get moving.
It's time to get fit.

Over-indulgence has made
my belly big.
I don't want to look like
a fat black pig.

Once I was slim;
I don't need a six-pack.
I'm too lazy for the gym,
but I want my flat tummy back.

I have to work hard for the
body that I want, though I
don't want to get all skinny,
looking gaunt.

The numbers on the scale are
creeping up higher; my stomach
looks like it's carrying a spare
tyre.

People often ask me, 'Oh, are you
expecting a baby?' I want to reply, 'No,
pie and rice, maybe, also vegetables,
chips, and lashings of gravy.'

I have my Nike trainers,
so I should just do it. I have the desire
and the determination.
No fear, not even a bit.

When the morning comes,
I'll be out walking, not in bed snoring.
I mean it, I'll be exercising.
I'm not just talking.

I see other people doing it,
jogging down the street, but for now
I'll just walk briskly, with my headphones on,
and with the music, I'll step to the beat.

I will work up a real sweat,
Does anybody want to bet?
Some say if you put a lot into life
Then a lot is what you will get.

On the menu are stomach crunches,
not big heavy lunches.
I know that I have to eat,
but not too many treats.

It's not just about looking good on the
outside; it's also about what's going on
inside. I want to be healthy; a person can
get sick even if they are wealthy.

I'm not getting any younger. I must be aware,
this body is mine, and I have to take care.
I will breathe better and see better,
walk better and talk better.

I want to train like an athlete.
I'm very serious. I want to push my body
to see how far it can go; I'm very
curious.

'Get fit,' I say to myself,
as I press snooze on the alarm for the last time.
Then I try to go back to sleep.
'Get fit,' I say. 'What you sow, you reap.'

Am I dreaming again, or what?
I'm supposed to be training.
No, I have not forgot. It's cold and it's raining;
it's not even hot.

Come on; come on, get up, get up.
Get fit, get fit, get fit.
Well, this is what I did: woke at 12, midday,
with cake and custard on the way.

This get fit stuff is tough,
though I'm being serious about wanting
to do this training. I'll do it till I'm done.
I will be number one.

I don't just want to wear the sports clothes
and then act as if nobody knows
that underneath it all
my toned stomach is actually like a massive ball.

Just do it properly. I will do it hopefully,
although it's not easy;
getting fit will please me.
Get fit!

44. 'Care Worker'

Your personality is cold.
That you'll grow old quickly
haven't you ever been told?
It's almost to the point of freezing.
You're unable to melt. I imagine
your heart to be like the toughest
burgundy-coloured leather, as you
look at me up and down and then
say to me, 'Oh whatever.'

Your sarcasm is incredibly blunt;
are you just putting on a front?
Your tongue is as sharp as a new razor blade
as you take a slice out of my emotions.
Then you try to cause a reaction and a commotion.
You try to wind me up like a clock, and I feel like
setting off the hospital fire alarm.
I don't plan on starting a fire, but I just wish
that you were older, so that you would retire.

You're so petite, and if I were to blow you
like a feather, you would probably end up
flying down the street.
If I were to touch you, you would break at my feet.
I will not react, but I know that
you will never get the sack.
Who is really sick, is it me or is it you?
I think that you need to be a patient, not a carer,
in this hospital too.

You were one of my carers when I was sick,
but just for the hospital records,
I'm not as soft or as thick as you think.
Though I'm also not as hard as you;
no way, I could never be that cruel.
There seems to be no care left in you. As you
strut your annoying stuff down the hospital corridor,
with your Spanish accent, I'd love to say to you,
'Where are your muscles, Ms Paella?'

I was really glad when I got better
and eventually left the ward.
You can keep your attitude,
and I'll keep mine.
I feel that somehow,
I beat you to the finishing line.
It's a small world, and one day we might meet,
though I really don't know if we would
ever shake hands and greet.

Me

45. Shine

◇ ◇ ◇ ◇◇◇◇ ◇ ◇

I want the real me to come
shining through the old me.
The real me is new; she's fresh and exciting.
She's happening right now.

Shine so brightly
that traces of my past
do not camouflage my present or my future.
Shine, so that people will see the love in me.

Radiate, blossom, and bloom;
Mature, sweet sunflower,
shine like never before.
Darkness will be removed and consumed.

Let the world see the beauty
that lies beneath my smooth,
golden chocolate-coloured skin.
People will see me rise and shine.

46. Fresh

◇ ⋈◇ ◇ ◇⋈◇ ◇

Fresh, wild, and free,
feeling really funky,
unique and rare individuality,
that's me.

Panache and style,
with my beautiful smile.
Quality assurance combined
with poetic performance.

State of the art, looking real smart.
Natural woman,
not made up, no make-up,
no wake up.

Talented, though quite often taken for granted;
strong minded yet humbled to the extent
of knowing that it's God
who gives me strength.

47. Being Me

Being me means learning to develop into the woman
God created me to be.
Being me means I'd rather not be anyone else
other than myself.
Being me means seeing and realising that I can aspire
to be a better individual every day.

I will be creative and try my best to be happy.
I will get fit and eventually get healthy.
Positive thinking is the key to help improve my capabilities.
I'll be ambitious and try to do as much as I can.
I'll refuse to let problems in the past influence my future,
because I was born to be a great and wonderful woman.

48. Misunderstood

◇◇◇ ◇◇◇ ◇◇◇ ◇◇◇ ◇ ◇◇◇ ◇◇

She's often misunderstood,
though she knows that she could
receive what she wants to achieve.

She plays to win,
and she has a thick skin.
Jesus is the king she believes in.

A born-again Christian,
she is on a mission
with a new transition.

Misunderstood,
though she gives no explanation
for being misunderstood.

Experience

49. In My Shoes

What would you do in my shoes?
Would you run, hop, skip, or jump?
I turned left; would you go right?
I was not out of my mind and had not lost my sight.

In my shoes, I took a risk.
I broke the chain and got things fixed.
In my shoes, would you have said yes?
Well, I said no, and then I had to go.

In my shoes, what would you have done?
Would you have given up before you had even begun?
I learned a lesson that made me stronger.
I now have the courage to go on for longer.

If you had faced the battle,
would you have gone on until the end?
Would you have climbed every hurdle and turned at every bend?
I achieved my mission whilst marching to that position.

In my shoes, would you have done the same?
We may have minds in common
though choose to play
a different game.

50. My View of the World

I feel the beauty, though I see the ugliness.
I taste the sweetness, though I can sense the bitterness.
I hear the melody, but I have felt the tragedy.

I live in the real world, which is full of make-believe.
I view the world, and the world views me;
why can't our views link in harmony?

I see progression, even though I have felt depression.
I feel the passion though refuse to follow fashion.
I have felt the pain and taken the strain.

My view of the world is not clouded;
although there are clouds in the sky,
I have none in my eyes.

I view the world.
I view what I see and see what I view;
at the same time, I feel it, too.

51. Backslidden Christian

You call yourself a Christian;
just take a look at what you've done.
Christian woman, Christian woman,
who do you think you are kidding?

You used to judge others, yes,
your own sisters and brothers;
now you are doing wrong, and
for how long?

Don't you realise
you are ruining your life?
Be a woman of integrity and virtue;
be honest and true.

Repent, repent, repent.
Get down on your knees;
cry out for God's mercy,
please, please, please!

How many times now
have you backslidden?
Oh, praise the Lord,
for He is very forgiving.

Learn from your mistakes,
no matter how long it takes.
Seek the Lord's face
and His amazing grace.

Life can be rough and tough,
though don't turn to all that bad stuff.
You know what I mean:
try to keep pure and clean.

Finish the race
that you started before;
don't even bother to go knocking
on the devil's door.

(Thank you, Jesus, for forgiving me.)

52. Further Education

Teacher, teacher, the teaching methods that you use
leave me feeling lost and confused.
With your degree and possible PhD,
I'm not learning from you; you're fooling me.

I went to college to learn something new;
now I know that good teachers are rare and few.
I have met some good ones, but not all are great.
I could teach a thing or two and hold a teaching debate.

I was so enthusiastic about gaining a new skill.
I was eager to learn; it was such a thrill.
Health and social care was the subject I wanted to do,
but the teachers had some kind of psychoanalytical attitude.

I became aware that they were all studying me.
It was like some major conspiracy theory.
Eventually, I left feeling sad and stressed.
I couldn't take anymore; I was total depressed.

It was in the year 2000 that all this happened to me.
However, after that I became a Christian eventually.
I gave my life to Jesus and accepted Him as my Saviour.
He's now my new teacher and friend; He's shown me favour.

53. Hospital Restraint Procedure

Did they know that when they held me down
to restrain me, that I would one day rise
and tell my story?

Did they know that the pain that they inflicted
upon me would help to make me the fighter
that I am today?

Did they know that they were abusing their positions
of power? Their so-called professional attitude
left me feeling used and abused.

Did they know that the restraint procedure they used
upon me would eventually lead to me having
victory?

54. The Colour that You Are

The colour that you are is more than just a shade.
It often depicts how
and where you were made.

Black or white, yellow or even dark blue,
the colour that you are
will always be you.

Some prefer to be dark while others prefer to be light,
though history has shown, that whether black or white,
people do not always have the same rights.

The colour that you are can take pride like a religion,
with values and tradition,
holding an important position.

Where you want to go and what you know can determine
the type of person you will become.
Your colour can have an influence on what you have done.

The colour that you are can run deep into the mind,
touching the heart and soul with a shade that is rich
and bold.

So do not take your colour for granted.
Be grateful for who you are, and think
about how your biological genetic seed was planted.

Don't let your colour determine who or what you will be.
Remember:
We were all born to be free!

55. Take a Look

Look at the past;
what do you see?
I remember you
standing next to me.

Look at the present;
what does it hold?
From where I am standing,
you now seem cold.

Look at the future;
what does it say?
It says that I will always
love you, anyway.

56. Feeling Emotional

The pain hurts.
I feel as though I'll burst.

The rain pours.
I refuse to stay indoors.

The shoes fit,
so I do not sit.

The sun shines.
I develop laughter lines.

I rise and fall
and then always stand up tall.

The taste is so sweet,
such a delicious treat.

The sound is music to my ears.
The melody brings me to tears.

London

57. The Londoner

'Good morning, London,'
I say to myself as I lock the front door behind me.
I'm ready to face the day.
It's raining, and the sky is grey,
but I'm used to this type of weather anyway.
Most people are not smiling;
they usually do, when the sun is shining.
The atmosphere is as hard and cold as the ground;
if I did not say hello to people first,
then they would not make a sound.

Born and bred in London Town, it's where I've lived the most;
this morning, it was all rush, rush, rush.
I had no time for toast.
I walk carefully, trying to dodge the dog poo,
in my new pair of shoes.
I stand in the cold at the bus stop, shivering, with eyes watering.
The packed bus comes along, but only one person is allowed on;
it's not me, so I continue to wait patiently.
Where am I going? I think to myself, as I stand with white vapour
coming out from my nose and breath.

A strange young man passes me by;
we acknowledge each other
and both say, 'Hi.'
He blows cigarette smoke right in my face
and ends up intruding in my space.
'Cheer up, love, it might never happen'
is what comes out of his mouth,
and then he gives me a cheeky grin
as he puts his cigarette butt in the bin.
The Londoner.

58. Space

I need my space.
Everywhere I go, people are always on my case,
right in my face; it's such a disgrace.
I want to get out of this rat race.
I want to go to a better place where I will feel safe
and never be traced.

What I really want is a taste of life
at a much slower pace.
I've thought of getting out of the country and
maybe going to another city.
At times it's hard to find peace on these London streets;
this town sometimes makes my heart skip a beat.

The disrespect; do they actually forget
that I am a human being, after all?
Sometimes I feel so small and can't walk properly;
I almost have to crawl.
I've taken many falls on these London streets,
physically, emotionally, even spiritually.

People think that they know me so well,
though it looks like they have hatred
in their eyes; I can tell.
London Town often gets me down.
These streets are mean to me; therefore,
I want to leave.

I feel as though I do not belong;
at times I feel weak and not strong.
Where can I go? What can I do?
Who on earth can I run to?
They are coming for me.
It's no joke; I have to flee.

I'm supposed to be free,
but I have nowhere on this earth to go to.
I'm just stuck in this hot public inferno.
Who can free me from this difficult life?
Who can help me to survive
so that I can stand up tall and never, ever fall?

Who can save me from death
so that I do not have to breathe my last breath?
Who can I depend on when all else fails?
Who will give me power and strength
and make me bold and brave?
Who will always be on my side?

I'm lost and in despair.
Many people in this troubled world look and stare,
but do they actually care? I have the answer; I have it for sure.
I found it when I knocked on heaven's door.
Someone made me feel welcome,
no harassment or discrimination.

It's Jesus who has set me free.
He has given me the ability to see.
Now I cry out to Jesus;
I know that He feeds us,
with spiritual food that is good for the soul.
I need my space, though I cling to the Lord's amazing grace.

59. British Summer Time

Here comes the sun.
Everybody, soak it up and catch the summer breeze,
because when winter comes, we might just freeze.
Rest beside the trees; the birds are resting too.
Strawberry ice cream, bursting with flavour;
there is one for me and one for you.

Flip-flops and vest tops;
no need for woollen socks.
Mini-skirts, shorts, and sunglasses;
people are giving each other secret glances.
The pollen count is as high as the sky.
Be careful not to get stung by the bee flying by.

Roses are in full bloom.
Cars drive fast on the road with rooftops down,
with drivers blasting favourite tunes.
Another year for Wimbledon. Well done, Andy Murray;
a wonderful achievement in 2013.
He really stirred up a flurry.

Longer days, hot nights, carnivals and fun fairs.
Barbeques are heating up.
Fruit punch is served in clear plastic cups.
Open air concerts and parks are packed,
bottles of water in shop fridges are stacked.
Sandy beaches, cream and peaches.

Lovers walk hand in hand;
children play in the sand.
How long will the hot sunshine last for?
Let's enjoy it, because in a couple of months,
cold weather is what's in store.
British summer time.

Africa

60. Black History

Has the real truth ever been told
about how my ancestors were sold?
When will racism and harassment
cease to go on, because of where
a person comes from?

My education taught me little about black history.
To me, the whole thing seems like a mystery.
I have to educate myself now.
It's not too late to learn something new.
Then I will be in a better position to know what is true.

I will aim to be a history-maker; my story will be told.
People will hear this black woman's voice,
both the young and the old.
I want to help stop discrimination
and be a role model for future generations.

My forefathers paved the way
Now I pray that I will get to the promised land one day.
The colour of my skin
will not determine my success.
Despite difficulties I've faced, I'm a winner nonetheless.

61. African Roots

I'm going
back to my roots,
a journey enriched
with truth.

My culture, the future, nature, nurture.
I'm going to where I belong;
a foreign land is where I come from.

My heritage from parentage,
mature vintage.
National identity, not false insecurity.

I'm going away to seek my treasure;
my buried history
I need to discover.

Dig deep within, the traveller destined to win.
I'm going, but will I return
with a fresh new outlook from what I have learned?

A deeper understanding of what life means;
I'm going back to my roots
to where I should be.

Family
history,
not slavery mentality.

I'm going to be free.
I'm going to be me.
Will Africa accept me?

62. Through the Eyes of an African Child

Through the eyes of an African child,
I see the innocence;
I see joy, I see pain, and sometimes I see frustration.
Why do they live in a difficult world without justification?

I see colour, I see shape, and I also see respect;
what you give in life is what you will get
I see that time will tell.
Will the child succeed in life and eventually do well?

Through the eyes of an African child,
I see strength and determination;
even though life can be tough,
it's possible to have aspirations.

I see injustice; I see improvement.
I see how far a nation has come.
I see how hard ancestors have worked.
I see what they have done and become.

Through the eyes of an African child,
I see culture and tradition;
I see that heritage has an important place
and an important position.

I see neglect; I see that people protect.
I see community spirit;
I see that lives are transformed when people stick together.
Bonds can be made forever.

Through the eyes of an African child,
I see powerful history;
I see evidence of struggle and the will to survive.
I see how people are often deprived.

I see past, I see present, I see a future too.
The eyes of an African child
make me realise
that there is something I must do.

63. The African

The African works hard for a living,
with much appreciation
for the little he or she is given.

The African lives in a land with resources that are many,
yet people continue to struggle,
and hunger pains are plenty.

The African has culture, mingled with tradition,
an inner strength that runs so deep
with hope and ambition.

The African has a heritage, the African has a soul.
The African has a will to survive;
the African has a goal.

64. Lights Out in Ghana

Darkness, you frighten me.
I lose the ability to see.
You surround me with nothing else but black.
It makes me feel as though I am under attack.

I lose all sense of direction,
then I pray to God,
'Help me.
Please give me protection.'

I scream and cry out,
'The Lord is my light and my salvation,
Whom shall I fear?'
I then feel a comforting presence drawing near.

God is never far away,
though it helps
if we pray,
without doubt, every day.

Miscellaneous

65. Justice

◇ ◇ ◇ ◇ ◇ ◇ ◇ ◇

To people of the world who are wrongly accused:
rise up, people,
for you know the truth.

To people of the world who have been abused:
don't give up on life;
your life is for life.

To people of the world who are confused:
stand tall
and do not be fooled.

To people of the world who have been used:
the past is past;
it's now up to you.

The accused,
the abused,
the confused, the used:

Your life is for you;
live it for you.
Be as free as you possibly can be.

Do not let another life ruin your one;
be happy to be you.
People like you are rare and few.

Always remember that whatever happened yesterday,
Does not need to happen today.
Believe that you will receive justice someday.

Oppressed people of the world:
have faith that a day will come
when you will no longer be over-powered.

All human beings
have their own individual power,
the power from within.

Oppressed people of the world:
rest assured that
the day will eventually come,

all accusers,
all abusers,
all confusers, all users

will be judged
for the wrong
that they have done.

66. Poetry in Motion

Rhythm
rhyme
spirit
chime.

Bongo
drum
in my
tum.

Faster
faster
no room
for disaster.

Poet,
know it
don't waste
It or blow it.

67. It's Beautiful Outside

I'm an outdoors type of girl, come rain or shine.
God saturates and drenches me with His blessings,
He's ever so kind.
With Jesus, the sun always shines.
There is never a dull moment;
even in the snow, I can walk an extra mile.

It's beautiful outside.
The sky is pure blue, and even if it were grey,
there's no way that I'm staying in today.
My stylish clothes are on, and my hair is done;
my bag is packed appropriately,
and I prepare to walk notably.

The ground beneath me seems like it's moving,
encouraging me to have an extra spring in my step.
I have been blessed with natural rhythm;
surely nothing or can get me upset.
I proceed to calmly walk down the London streets,
absorbing the fresh air, with its natural aroma.

There are people everywhere, enjoying the time and space;
right now I'm glad to be here, in such an amazing place.
I never walk alone; Jesus always walks by my side.
He always leads the way and is also able to guide.
I have no particular destination on this occasion.
I walk feeling free; where the spirit of the Lord is, there is liberty.

I begin to ponder, should I go somewhere specific or not?
Maybe I should go to some popular new place in town,
where there are artists like me, who are prolific.
I continue on with my journey;
at the moment, there is no need to rest, because
walking is one of the things that I like to do best.

Supermarkets, restaurants, and shops galore:
there's a lot more to see
if I were to go into a store, I'm sure.
I like to shop; I really do,
though today is just for walking,
until there is nowhere left to walk to.

Strangers pass me by; I smile and say hello,
though there is no time for a chat, because
I have somewhere to walk to, as a matter of fact.
Time seems to be moving slowly, which is lovely
because I'm in no hurry.
I am sensitive to the environment; I love the climate.

It must look as though I have blessed written all over my face.
Where to now, what direction should I take?
I don't need to worry about arriving somewhere too late.
I may go to the park and be surrounded by flowers and green grass.
Maybe read my favourite book, sing, dance, and pray.
Just enjoy this special occasion, on a fantastic day like today.

Suddenly I stop; I can't think where to go to anymore.
I have come to a standstill, though my feet are not even sore.
It's such a big world with lots to see;
there are many people around me.
Where do I go?
What do I do?

I'm not far from home, so I turn around;
however, I stop yet again and think to myself,
Where are all my friends?
Tears begin to well up in my eyes.
I take small steps back to my empty house.
It's beautiful outside.

68. Creation

Charles Darwin's theory of evolution
versus the notion of God's creation.
Let us analyse both ideas with thorough
examination and exploration.
According to the Bible, in the beginning,
God created the heavens and the earth,
though according to Charles Darwin,
there was a Big Bang, and we evolved
from monkeys at birth.
Were we made in God's own image,
or were there apes in our lineage?

Do we believe
in Adam and Eve
or in natural selection?
How or what do we perceive?
There are controversies surrounding the debate
of the world's creation,
whether subjective or objective,
with or without speculation.
Darwin's *The Descent of Man,*
or the Almighty God being the one
with the master plan?

69. The Race

Run like you've got fire in your feet girl,
'cos ain't nobody gonna catch you
when you run like you've been trained too.
Run like Usain Bolt,
because you know it wasn't your fault.

They'll never catch you, even if they try.
If there's justice to be had,
then it's coming your way.
Don't worry about what your enemies might say.
Their jealousy will destroy them and you'll beat them one day.

Walk if you have to, but run when you can.
You've got pure strength within you.
Yeah, you can beat the toughest man.
Run the race at your own pace,
so that you don't fall flat on your face.

70. Confronting the Enemy

Enough! If you push me again, metaphorically speaking,
I might just explode in your face, though I would not
want to bring upon myself shame and disgrace.

The provocation and disrespect;
do you not know that I can give as well as I get?
And before I forget:

The Lord executes righteousness and justice
to all who are oppressed.
Do you remember how you made me stressed?

When I shed tears, you hardly made a sound.
Now I'm getting much more bolder.
I once was lost but now I'm found.

You keep on pushing and keep on being cruel,
but just bear in mind, that I will ignite the build-up
of fuel. The fire will burn within me, and I will shine brightly.

What you are doing is not right,
so I have to defend myself and put up a fight,
not physically, spiritually and with all my might.

I haven't come this far for nothing.
I'm determined to succeed.
God gives me strength and provides my every need.

I will continue to persevere and to be optimistic.
My head is not too high in the clouds; I will be realistic.
I have power from within, because of the joy God brings.

Why do you play this game and cause me so much pain?
I don't need to mention your name,
but do you not feel any shame?

And just for the record, I want to make myself clear:
Don't even attempt to try me again, do you hear?
I've had about as much as I can take; now I have no fear.

Yes, I am different from you,
but what's with the negative attitude?
Why do you treat me like I'm some kind of fool?

This poem goes out to all who have left me with emotional scars.
The pain that I have endured has only made me stronger.
Now I can keep on keeping on and go on for longer.

I will continue to show love, no matter what you do or say.
It is the Almighty God who taught me to behave this way.
One last thing that I want to say:

Who are you anyway?

71. Dreamer

◇ ◇◇◇◇ ◇◇ ◇◇◇◇ ◇◇ ◇

I'm dreaming when I wake,
wanting to escape.
I'm falling when I rise;
vivid images fill closed eyes.
I'm running with acceleration,
without any real destination.
I'm swimming in an ocean;
I'm cold when I'm warm.

In the darkness there is light;
through the blindness there is sight.
Great mystery always surrounds the night.
There are strangers in my dreams
and places not yet seen.
The past, the present, and the future I see too.
I'm flying in the sky.
I can almost feel the colour blue.

I'm not lost for words;
when I sleep, I talk.
Briskly I walk.
I can smell the flavours and taste the aroma;
can others in my dreams see my true persona?
I wake but want to sleep some more;
these dreams are astounding.
I want to explore.

Eventually I awaken
as I sink back into reality,
forgetting what was imaginary normality.
Some memories still linger
and play on my mind.
The good dreams I want to remember.
Nightmares can vanish and never be seen again.
I'm still dreaming when I wake and hope remains.

72. A Different Shade of Blue

A different shade of blue
was the sky throughout the day;
pastel coloured in the morning,
the palest blue yet to date.
Mingled with white clouds in places
gave a bright, light, heavenly feel.

By afternoon the sky had changed,
though a wonderful shade of blue remained.
Far away, in the distance,
the sky seemed white from my view.
A tint of grey showed a type of misty foggy haze,
mysterious looking and thought provoking.

If I were to travel to that distance which I can see,
would the shade of blue be different,
if that part of the sky was above me?
Though by the time that I had travelled
to that particular place, I may not see
that same blue face to face.

Movement does take place up above,
as it does to down below.
If I go in search of the mysterious blue
piece of sky, it may have other places to go.
By the time I get there, I may not see
what I had expected.

It's quite exciting
not knowing what shade will be waiting.
Actually, I do not think that I need to travel;
I'm beginning to like the mysterious blue
feeling which I have.
Mystery leads me to use my imagination;

The mysterious blue:
that sounds real cool.
I imagine cool being a shade of blue.
Later that day, things had not changed.
The sky was still the same; close to me,
what I could see was calm and so serene.

Pale blue and bright, a fantastic sight,
though I knew that it would soon be night.
In the distance, the mystery remained;
meanwhile, I continued waiting patiently
to see the colours change.
Seeing so much blue is what I'm now used to.

By early evening, change occurred.
There were no clouds in the air;
therefore, I continued to stare.
As time went on,
the clock moved. Within an hour,
I am sure that I could see a change in colour.

The distant mystery that I decided to leave to
my imagination then transformed into
light pink, or was it orange?
A contrasting combination.
It was too far for me to be certain,
in order for me to clarify.

Was it reality, or was something deceiving my eyes?
I continued to wait for the next change
that I knew would be soon approaching.
Then it appeared, layer upon layer,
different shades of blue.
Look at what the sky has proved it can do.

Next came late evening,
with the darkness proceeding;
lightness was on its way out.
A strange shade of blue, a touch of turquoise,
a hint of purple or green
I'm sure is what I saw.

The next shade was dark blue,
shades of brown gave
off a rustic, rugged mood.
Was it the street lighting which gave that effect?
The bright sparkling glows
piercing to the sky direct.

Was it a false colour?
How am I to discover?
Nevertheless, the sky remained
a different shade of blue.
Blue.
Blue.
Blue.

73. Emily Brontë

No cowardly soul was she;
it was plain for the world to see.
Strong she stood, and few wrote
like she could.
A real inspiration, as I read
Emily Brontë's poetry with great
fascination. My heart is filled with
pleasure, and her poems, I will treasure.

A true heroine to me; she wrote with
great intensity. Superbly intriguing and
breathtaking. An intrepid style of writing,
with her eminence and great reverence.
Classic English literature at its best.
Into the hall of fame, Emily's poetry
has passed the test, and many will remember
her name.

A creative imagination that included fact
and fiction. She expressed herself in a simple
way by what she would write and say.
Great emphasis was placed on nature, and she
lived in the beautiful surroundings of Yorkshire.
With her enchanting poetry,
she gently manages
to draw the reader into her territory.

Illustrious with a strong sense of faith,
also courageous, bold, and brave.
Initially she hid her true identity and name,
though she beat the men at their own game.
Sometimes she wrote about joy and light
and at other times about death and night.
Emily used conflict, contrast, and at times metaphor;
she is a woman I admire, strongly applaud, and adore.

74. Valerie

It was me who found Valerie's cold, stiff
purple dead body on the hospital bedroom floor.
I rushed to tell the staff; they didn't seem surprised.
Had they somehow known about it before?
Their attitude was so relaxed.
I was in shock at the time and did not stop to think
how she died; what was the exact reason?

It was only the day before that Valerie and I had both
been speaking; she came to return my phone charger.
I never realised that I would not see her again.
It's sad because we became very good friends.
Now I often think of Valerie and the way she used to be.
Unfortunately, she's no longer with us, and her face I can
no longer see. Rest in peace, Valerie.

75. Vegan Diet

Give me vegetables to eat.
No pig meat or horse and no cow's feet.
Carrots, cabbage, courgettes, and sweet corn.
Potatoes, plantains, and yams: I eat them all.

Nice, well-cooked veg, no red, rare blood-dripping flesh.
A vegan diet is what I strongly suggest.
I'll have soya milk, not 'moo' milk squeezed from animal teats.
I can't even look at jellied eels, please.

I haven't always eaten a vegan diet; as a
child, I was brought up on meat.
Chicken wings and burgers used to be my favourite treats.
Now I cannot eat something that was once alive.
I've found a new way of living and a better way to survive.

No eggs for breakfast.
No cheese and onion quiche for lunch.
Liver for supper is out,
without a doubt.

No turkey at Christmas; I much prefer a nut roast.
No corned beef in my sandwich;
no bacon on my toast.
I don't mind marmite on my bread, strictly pure veg.

76. Heaven

One day, I hope to go to heaven,
and see the Lord face to face.
I've heard that heaven is a beautiful place.
I'll see my Wonderful Counsellor,
my heavenly father.

Will I see my fellow sisters and brothers?
When I get to the promised land.
Will my family be there?
Including those who have passed away.
I hope that we will all get to heaven, to God I pray.

There's so much trouble in the world,
but I believe that one day
there'll be heaven on earth.
We will all eventually get
what we deserve.

I also believe that there's a hell.
But if we manage to do well,
then we'll get to a much better place,
with the love and power
of God's amazing grace.

77. Who Is to Blame?

Who's to blame? I ask myself.
Who started this whole thing?
Who should be made to stand accused
and held responsible?
All the fighting,
all the backbiting;
what is it all for?
Let's put an end to things,
make amends, and aim to fight no more.
If anyone is to blame,
then I say that it is God.
It began years ago when He created the world.

If people want to investigate who is to blame,
if people want to fight about who is to blame,
if people feel that they have the right to know who is to blame,
if people want my view about who is to blame,
my theory is that it is God,
for He is the creator and the answer.
Though let this whole thing be put into a fair perspective
and examine it carefully.
It's important for me to make myself clear
so that people will fully understand me.
We need to realise that God's son, Jesus Christ, was crucified
and died, to save our lives.

He was nailed to the cross, and His dignity was lost.
He felt pain, and He felt shame.
However, He was able to rise again.
When things go wrong, people are often quick to judge
and sometimes point their finger.
When things are going right,
well then, it's all right.

It's not wrong, so what's the problem?
The problem is, I now realise that the good in the world
is quite often taken for granted.
There is more good than bad in this world,
though people often accuse God of allowing people to suffer.

I say, if people are accused of doing the wrong thing,
take a look at the good they have done
and the joy that they bring.
Make Him stand accused;
let Him be judged.
Then bring forth witnesses to the stand;
let testimonies be given
and a verdict be made.
Let a date be set for judgement day.
Who is to blame?
I say the Lord
in Jesus' name!

78. The Truth and Lies

It began long ago,
far, far away in a land which had no name.
The Truth had not yet been born, but the Lies had,
and many said that things would remain the same.
The Lies began quite small,
and as they were fed, they matured.
With appropriate training, they grew to be strong and tall.
They trained both day and night;
it was not long before they became fit and healthy.
Eventually, they began to get rich and wealthy.
The Lies ruled the land with their mighty power;
they spread and settled, with growth maintained hour by hour.

Then one day, a traveller came to town,
going by the name of Truth.
He came from a completely different area;
it could be said that he was a foreigner.
The Lies looked on as they saw the Truth approaching,
and they began to shout,
'Get back, get back, or we will attack.'
The Truth lifted up its arms,
continued moving forwards, and then said,
'I come in the name of Jesus Christ.'
The Lies looked at each other and then at the Truth;
they had no understanding, but they decided what to do.

'Away, away, away with you.
Our land is full of lies,'
they shouted.
'Away, away, away with you,
We have no room for truth.
Go back, right back to wherever you come from.
There is no room for you here, and you do not belong.

If your name is called Truth, we are called Lies.'
'The two cannot mix, in our eyes.'
The Truth shouted,
'Your eyes are blind; you do not see.
If you could, you would see me clearly.'

'Get back, get back, get back we say,' the Lies replied,
if you want live to see another real day.
Don't even bother to get down on your knees to pray.
Do not come any nearer; it's for your own good.
Our Lies will cause you great harm, if you refuse to do as you should.'
The Truth laughed and said,
'Look, you need to realise that eventually harm will come to you.
Please be willing to accept me as the Truth.
Your Lies will destroy all of your lives,
if that is what your lying land is used to.
Believe what I say, my name is called Truth.
The truth is what you should believe; it will really help you.'

'Accept me as a friend,
Do not be quick and ready to defend.
What I have should not offend you.
Let me live amongst you
so that I can show you that the Truth can make a positive difference.
Let me walk, let me talk, let me preach, let me teach.
Let me give to you my Truth.
I cannot pretend, and I will not comprehend.
I realise that I am completely different from you.
I will continue to be persistent, because you all show much resistance.
My name is called Truth, Truth I tell you.
I can help free your lying minds.'

'Enough, enough, enough, that's more than
enough,' the Lies screamed.
'No more of your sweet talking. Get back.'
In great numbers, the Lies started walking.
Strong and bold, both young and old, the Lies started to unfold.
The Truth became quite weak; it was obvious to see.
'Please, please,' the Truth cried, 'do not harm me with your Lies.
Yes, it is true that you are stronger than me.
I am small, and that cannot be denied.
You were all here before me, and I realise that I am new to your land.
However, I have come here on a mission. I have God's permission.
It also includes great plans.'

The Lies grew annoyed and then became very angry.
They then began to show their fury.
'Lord, have mercy upon their souls,' cried out the Truth.
'There is so much evil present here, from what I can feel and see.
I think the devil must be living here for free.
If he does, then the truth needs to be told,
and right now, it can only come from me.
Truth is my name, I tell you again, and I do not have a surname.
I am the Truth, the whole Truth, and nothing but the Truth,
And you should all feel ashamed.'
The Truth saw that the Lies were becoming quite hot;
the pressure was now on.

The Truth stood alone; however, it had power and experience to know,
that when the Truth is told, those Lies, however bold,
they will eventually run for cover.
The Lies began to shake; they then began to tremble,
while the Truth stood confident and bold.
Hotter and hotter the Lies became, as they began to sweat.
'Liar, liar, look: your pants are on fire,'
cried out the Truth.
'Liar, liar, I say your pants are on fire.'

Black, stinking smoke came out from their behinds.
The Lies could not take the Truth anymore;
they had simply had enough.

They gathered together, and at this stage,
things started to get rough.
'We warned you,' said the Lies, 'but you would not listen.
We will now put an end to your so-called truthful mission.
An end to your Truth; we will keep our Lies,
You keep what is right, and we will choose to remain blind.'
The Lies ran forward and pounced on the Truth,
and the Truth was then killed.
But as they ran, one Lie tripped and fell;
that Lie was also killed as well.
Side by side lay the Truth with a Lie;
they were both dead and unable to rise.

The Lies looked at each other
and then at the ground;
one shouted,
'Lord, what have we done?
We killed the Truth but in doing so,
we killed one of our own.
One of our Lies is lying on the ground.
He makes no sound at all.'
'It's true, it's true, oh, it's true,' another Lie said.
'We killed them both, and we killed the Truth.
So it was all true, the story
that the Truth had been telling us.

'The Truth did say that there would come a day,
when our Lies would eventually destroy all of our lives.
Now one of us lays down, dead, next to the Truth,
by which it was led.'
'It's true, it's true,' they all began to say.

'We need to stop living our lying lives.
We have learned from the Truth that came here to teach us.
We have learned from the Truth that came here to preach to us.
We will change, our Lies cannot remain,
And we cannot destroy each other.
Our land will be transformed, and we will be reborn.
The Truth will remain here forever.'

'Glory Hallelujah!'
they shouted as they decided to celebrate.
They wasted no time,
for there was no time like the present;
the party was in honour of the Truth.
The Lies raised their hands and begun to feel their spirit;
they then danced like never before.
They had no choice, but to rejoice,
repent, and tell lies no more.
Some of the Lies fell to the floor,
though they did not stay there for long.
Some sang songs, and others were fully transformed.

Others wept, for they had many regrets.
'Our lies, all of our Lies caused us to sin.
Because we were so many, we thought we could win.
We killed the Truth, whom we did not know.
We gave it no chance, and before it died, we told it to go.
Mercy, mercy, Lord, have mercy upon our lying souls.
We admit that we have been lying and living in a lying land.'
They all agreed and knew that it was the right thing to do;
they would speak and live by the Truth. Days and months passed,
and that old lying land did not last, like it once had. All because of
the Truth, which one day came to visit and made the Lies realise
when the Truth is told, even if it is unknown, it cannot be denied.

So that lying land did not remain the same;
in fact, it completely changed.
The Truth spread around so fast, and those Lies disappeared;
honesty had been grasped at last.
Never again did anyone tell a lie
for fear that they might die.
There was now real love
in the community,
with trust and no insecurity.
Everyone knew what it meant
to love thy neighbour
and to show each other courtesy and favour.